I Can See

The Old Testament

Supported by St Andrew's Church,

Reading Street, Broadstairs

Maxine Gregory
and
Sabena J Hawthorne

Matador
9 Priory Business Park,
Wistow Road, Kibworth Beauchamp,
Leicestershire. LE8 0RX
Tel: 0116 279 2299
Email: books@troubador.co.uk
Web: www.troubador.co.uk/matador
Twitter: @matadorbooks

ISBN 978 1785890 376

British Library Cataloguing in Publication Data.
A catalogue record for this book is available from the British Library.

Printed and bound in Malta by Gutenberg Press Ltd
Typeset by Troubador Publishing Ltd, Leicester, UK

Matador is an imprint of Troubador Publishing Ltd

This book belongs to

Oliver, Catherine & William

December 2015

If I look carefully I can see...

Adam and Eve hiding behind a tree.

While Adam and Eve point at a snake that seems to gloat,

I can see Noah through the clearing building a big boat.

While Noah casts off to sea with his noisy, smelly load,

I can see old Sarah with Abraham walking down the road.

While Sarah whoops for joy as her belly grows bigger and bigger,

I can see Joseph being dragged off by his brothers who snigger.

While Joseph considers seven brawny cows, then seven scrawny,

I can see a baby amongst the reeds that grow tall and tawny.

While the baby squirms in his basket and begins to cry,

I can see a pharaoh standing under a locust filled sky.

While the pharaoh gallops through the desert after his slaves,

I can see Moses parting a sea of raging waves.

While Moses climbs Mount Sinai and writes on slabs of stone,

I can see Ruth clinging to Naomi with a heartfelt moan.

While Ruth bends down in foreign fields to pick the grain,

I can see Samuel stirring in his sleep again and again.

While Samuel points out to Eli that his sons are being bad,

I can see the giant Goliath shaking his huge fist like mad.

While Goliath is slain by David who is small but bold,

I can see the Queen of Sheba with camels, spices and gold.

While the Queen of Sheba praises King Solomon for being wise,

I can see Naboth in the vineyard under sunny skies.

While Naboth is pulled away, with Jezebel looking on,

I can see Esther pacing outside the palace, trying to be strong.

While Esther saves her people by facing the fierce king,

I can see Isaiah in a temple with angels who sing.

While Isaiah goes through the villages with messages of love,

I can see Jeremiah under the almond tree, viewing the blossom above.

While Jeremiah watches a potter shape and remould his clay,

I can see Daniel in the lion's den kneeling down to pray.

While Daniel is helped out of the den completely unharmed,

I can see Jonah sailing through a storm looking most alarmed.